Building Autonomous AI Agents with LangGraph

A Developer's Guide

Written By

Maxime Lane

Building Autonomous AI Agents with LangGraph: A Developer's Guide

Copyright

© 2025 Maxime Lane. All rights reserved.

Table of Contents

Preface

Have you ever marveled at how your favorite apps seem to understand your needs, or wondered what magic powers self-driving cars and intelligent chatbots? What if you could build a system that not only makes decisions on its own but also learns and adapts over time—one that transforms a simple idea into a dynamic, real-world solution? ***Building Autonomous AI Agents with LangGraph: A Developer's Guide*** is your gateway to that exciting frontier.

Imagine a world where a customer support agent handles thousands of inquiries simultaneously, offering personalized assistance 24/7 without a single coffee break. Picture an intelligent data analysis system that sifts through vast oceans of information in real time, uncovering insights that drive business strategies and innovation. These aren't distant dreams— they're the realities you can create using autonomous AI agents powered by LangGraph.

In this book, I will take you on a hands-on journey through the vibrant world of autonomous systems. You'll discover how to harness the power of graph-based AI to build agents that are not only smart but also incredibly efficient and scalable. We start from the basics, laying a solid foundation with graph theory and the inner workings of LangGraph. Then, through clear, step-by-step examples and real-world case studies, you'll see how these concepts come alive in applications that handle customer interactions and analyze complex data sets.

But this isn't just another technical manual filled with abstract theories and endless lines of code. We've woven in engaging stories and practical examples that mirror challenges and successes from today's tech landscape. Whether you're a seasoned developer eager to dive into the nuances of autonomous agents, or a curious innovator ready to experiment with cutting-edge technology, this guide is crafted to spark your creativity and fuel your passion.

By the time you finish this book, you'll not only understand how to build and optimize your own autonomous AI agents with LangGraph—you'll be empowered to push the boundaries of what's possible in your own projects. And once you've experienced the thrill of seeing your code transform into a smart, autonomous system, you'll want to share your journey with others. I invite you to revisit these pages, leave a review, and spark conversations with fellow developers about the future of AI.

Welcome to a world where innovation meets autonomy. Let's get started on building the next generation of intelligent systems together!

Chapter 1: Introduction

Welcome to *Building Autonomous AI Agents with LangGraph: A Developer's Guide.* In this chapter, we will explore the growing importance of autonomous AI agents, introduce LangGraph and its evolution, and explain who will benefit most from this guide. Whether you are a developer new to autonomous systems or someone looking to deepen your practical understanding, this chapter lays the foundation for everything that follows.

1.1 The Rise of Autonomous AI Agents

Autonomous AI agents are systems that can operate independently to perform tasks, make decisions, and adapt to changing environments without continuous human intervention. In today's fast-paced digital world, these agents have become integral in various industries and applications due to several key drivers:

- **Efficiency and Scalability:** Autonomous agents can manage repetitive or data-intensive tasks 24/7, reducing human workload and increasing efficiency.
- **Real-Time Decision Making:** With the integration of advanced machine learning and data processing techniques, these agents can analyze large volumes of data and make decisions in real time.
- **Personalization:** In customer-facing applications, autonomous agents can tailor responses and services based on user behavior, leading to improved customer satisfaction.
- **Innovation in Automation:** Industries like finance, healthcare, automotive, and customer service are leveraging autonomous agents to innovate and stay competitive.

Below is a table summarizing some common application areas of autonomous AI agents and their impact:

Application Area	Example	Impact
Customer Support	Chatbots & Virtual Assistants	Provide 24/7 support, reduce waiting times, and increase efficiency in handling inquiries.

Application Area	Example	Impact
Data Analysis	Automated Analytics Agents	Process vast amounts of data quickly, generating insights and predictions for better decision-making.
Autonomous Vehicles	Self-Driving Cars	Enhance road safety and efficiency by reducing human error in driving.
Healthcare	Diagnostic Agents	Assist in early detection of diseases and support personalized treatment plans.

The rapid evolution of technology has made it possible for these agents to learn from their environment and improve over time. This adaptability is largely driven by advancements in machine learning, natural language processing (NLP), and big data analytics. As these technologies mature, we see a shift from simple rule-based systems to sophisticated, autonomous agents capable of complex tasks.

1.2 Introducing LangGraph

LangGraph is a powerful framework designed to help developers build and manage autonomous AI agents by leveraging graph-based representations of data and logic. Its development was motivated by the need for more intuitive and flexible systems that can model complex relationships in data and agent behavior.

A Brief History and Evolution

Originally, many AI systems were built on traditional relational databases and static decision trees. However, as the complexity of tasks increased, it became clear that a more dynamic and interconnected approach was needed. LangGraph emerged as a solution to this challenge by:

- **Adopting Graph Theory:** By representing data as nodes and edges, LangGraph allows developers to capture intricate relationships and dependencies that traditional methods may overlook.
- **Enhancing Flexibility:** The modular architecture of LangGraph makes it easier to integrate various AI components, such as machine learning models and NLP tools.

- **Simplifying Complexity:** LangGraph abstracts much of the underlying complexity, enabling developers to focus on the logic and behavior of their autonomous agents rather than getting bogged down by low-level implementation details.

Core Principles of LangGraph

- **Modularity:** LangGraph's architecture is built on small, interchangeable modules. This design makes it easy to extend functionality and customize solutions.
- **Scalability:** Whether you're building a small prototype or a large-scale production system, LangGraph is designed to handle growing datasets and increasing agent complexity.
- **Interoperability:** LangGraph is designed to work seamlessly with popular AI libraries and frameworks, making it a flexible tool in a developer's toolkit.

A Simple Example

To illustrate how LangGraph works, let's look at a simple code snippet that creates a basic graph structure:

```python
# Import the LangGraph module
import langgraph

# Create a new graph instance
graph = langgraph.Graph()

# Add nodes to the graph
graph.add_node("Start")
graph.add_node("Process Data")
graph.add_node("Make Decision")

# Connect the nodes with edges to define the flow
graph.add_edge("Start", "Process Data")
graph.add_edge("Process Data", "Make Decision")

# Display the graph structure
print("Graph Nodes:", graph.nodes)
print("Graph Edges:", graph.edges)
```

Explanation of the Code:

- **Importing the Module:** We begin by importing the `langgraph` module, which contains all the necessary tools to create and manage our graph.
- **Creating a Graph Instance:** A new graph is instantiated using `langgraph.Graph()`.
- **Adding Nodes:** Nodes represent distinct steps or states in the autonomous agent's workflow. In this example, we add nodes for starting the process, processing data, and making decisions.
- **Connecting Nodes:** Edges are used to define the relationship or flow between nodes. Here, we connect "Start" to "Process Data" and then "Process Data" to "Make Decision".
- **Displaying the Structure:** Finally, the structure of the graph is printed, showing both nodes and the connections between them.

This example demonstrates how LangGraph can be used to model the logical flow of an autonomous agent in a clear and modular fashion.

1.3 Who This Book Is For

This guide is tailored for developers who are interested in building autonomous AI agents and want to strike a balance between theoretical knowledge and hands-on practical implementation. Here's what you can expect:

- **Practical Implementation:** We focus on real-world examples and case studies that you can follow along with and apply to your own projects.
- **Step-by-Step Guidance:** Each section provides detailed, incremental steps to ensure you understand not just what to do, but why you're doing it.
- **Developer-Friendly Language:** The content is written in clear, accessible language. Complex ideas are broken down into manageable parts, making it easier to grasp even if you're not an expert in graph theory or AI.
- **Comprehensive Coverage:** From setting up your development environment to advanced optimization techniques, this book covers

all the stages of building and deploying autonomous AI agents with LangGraph.

- **Community and Collaboration:** Beyond the code, you will learn about best practices, common pitfalls, and strategies to leverage the LangGraph community for continuous learning and improvement.

If you are a developer looking to enhance your skills in autonomous AI and are excited about working with cutting-edge tools like LangGraph, then this book is designed with you in mind. Whether you are building a prototype or deploying a full-scale system, the insights and hands-on examples provided here will serve as a valuable resource on your journey.

Chapter 2: Setting Up Your Environment

Before diving into building autonomous AI agents with LangGraph, it's essential to set up a reliable and efficient development environment. In this chapter, we'll cover everything from hardware and software prerequisites to installing LangGraph and configuring your system for your first run. We'll also discuss recommended development tools and best practices that will help you maintain a smooth workflow throughout your project.

2.1 Prerequisites and Installation

A well-prepared environment ensures that you can focus on coding without encountering unexpected issues. In this section, we will outline the necessary hardware and software requirements and walk you through the installation process.

Hardware Requirements

While LangGraph is designed to run on most modern development machines, having the right hardware can improve performance, especially when dealing with complex computations or large datasets. Below is a table summarizing the recommended hardware requirements:

Component	Minimum Requirement	Recommended
Processor (CPU)	Dual-core processor	Quad-core or higher
Memory (RAM)	4 GB	8 GB or more
Storage	10 GB free disk space	20 GB+ SSD for faster read/write speeds
Internet	Stable internet connection	Broadband connection

Software Requirements

To get started, you will need to have several software components installed on your machine. Below is a table summarizing the key software requirements:

Software	Version/Notes	Purpose
Operating System	Windows, macOS, or Linux	Host OS for development
Python	Python 3.7 or higher	Primary programming language
Pip	Latest version recommended	Python package installer
Virtual Environment Tool	`venv` (built into Python) or `virtualenv`	Isolating project dependencies
Git	Latest stable version	Version control and code collaboration

Installing LangGraph and Dependencies

1. **Install Python:**
   If you haven't installed Python yet, download the latest version (Python 3.7 or above) from python.org. Follow the installation instructions specific to your operating system. During installation, ensure that you check the option to add Python to your system's PATH.
2. **Set Up a Virtual Environment:**
   It's a good practice to create a virtual environment for your project to manage dependencies effectively. Open your terminal or command prompt and run:

```bash

# Create a new virtual environment in a folder
named 'env'
python -m venv env

# Activate the virtual environment
# On Windows:
env\Scripts\activate
```

```
# On macOS and Linux:
source env/bin/activate
```

3. **Upgrade pip:**
   Before installing any packages, ensure that your package installer is up to date:

   bash

   ```
   pip install --upgrade pip
   ```

4. **Install LangGraph:**
   Assuming LangGraph is available on PyPI, install it using pip:

   bash

   ```
   pip install langgraph
   ```

5. **Install Additional Dependencies:**
   Depending on your project requirements, you may need to install other packages (e.g., libraries for data processing or machine learning). For example:

   bash

   ```
   pip install numpy pandas scikit-learn
   ```

After executing these commands, LangGraph and its dependencies should be installed and ready for use.

2.2 Configuration and First Run

With LangGraph installed, the next step is to configure your project and verify that everything is working as expected.

Configuration Files

Many projects benefit from using configuration files to manage settings such as logging levels, data paths, or module options. LangGraph projects might use configuration files in JSON, YAML, or even Python modules. Below is an example of a simple YAML configuration file named `config.yaml`:

```yaml
# config.yaml
logging:
  level: INFO
  file: langgraph.log

graph:
  default_layout: "spring"
  max_nodes: 100

agent:
  name: "AutonomousAgent"
  behavior_mode: "adaptive"
```

Explanation:

- **Logging:** Specifies the logging level (e.g., INFO, DEBUG) and the file where logs should be saved.
- **Graph Settings:** Configures the default layout for graph visualization and sets a limit on the number of nodes.
- **Agent Settings:** Defines basic parameters for your autonomous agent, such as its name and behavior mode.

Loading the Configuration in Your Project

Here's a sample Python code snippet that demonstrates how to load and use this configuration file:

```python
import yaml
import langgraph

# Load the configuration file
with open('config.yaml', 'r') as file:
    config = yaml.safe_load(file)
```

```python
# Set up logging based on the configuration
import logging
logging.basicConfig(
    filename=config['logging']['file'],
    level=getattr(logging,
config['logging']['level']),
    format='%(asctime)s - %(levelname)s -
%(message)s'
)
logging.info("Configuration loaded successfully.")

# Initialize a LangGraph instance with parameters
from the config file
graph =
langgraph.Graph(layout=config['graph']['default_lay
out'])

print("Graph initialized with layout:",
config['graph']['default_layout'])
```

Explanation of the Code:

- The configuration file `config.yaml` is loaded using the `yaml` module.
- Logging is configured based on settings defined in the file.
- A LangGraph instance is initialized with parameters (e.g., graph layout) specified in the configuration.

Verifying Your Installation

To verify that LangGraph and all configurations are correctly set up, you can run a simple script that prints the current graph structure or configuration details. Create a file named `verify_setup.py` with the following content:

```python
python

import langgraph
import yaml

# Load configuration
```

```python
with open('config.yaml', 'r') as file:
    config = yaml.safe_load(file)

# Initialize a simple graph
graph =
langgraph.Graph(layout=config['graph']['default_lay
out'])
graph.add_node("Start")
graph.add_node("Process")
graph.add_edge("Start", "Process")

print("Graph Nodes:", graph.nodes)
print("Graph Edges:", graph.edges)
```

Run this script from your terminal:

```bash
bash

python verify_setup.py
```

You should see an output listing the nodes and edges, confirming that LangGraph is functioning as expected.

2.3 Development Tools and Best Practices

A well-equipped development environment is crucial for building reliable, maintainable, and scalable AI applications. In this section, we cover recommendations for integrated development environments (IDEs), version control, debugging tools, and testing frameworks.

IDE Recommendations

Choosing the right IDE can boost your productivity by providing helpful features such as syntax highlighting, code completion, and integrated debugging. Here are two popular IDEs for Python development:

- **Visual Studio Code (VSCode):**
    - o **Pros:** Lightweight, highly customizable, and a vast marketplace of extensions.

- o **Extensions:** Python extension by Microsoft, YAML support, GitLens for version control.
  - o **Getting Started:** Download from Visual Studio Code.
- **PyCharm:**
  - o **Pros:** Powerful features tailored for Python, robust refactoring tools, integrated testing support.
  - o **Community Edition:** Free and sufficient for most development tasks.
  - o **Getting Started:** Download from JetBrains PyCharm.

Version Control with Git

Using a version control system like Git is essential for tracking changes, collaborating with others, and maintaining a history of your code. Here's a quick guide to initializing a Git repository for your LangGraph project:

1. **Initialize Git:**

```bash
git init
```

2. **Add Your Files:**

```bash
git add .
```

3. **Commit Your Changes:**

```bash
git commit -m "Initial commit: Set up LangGraph environment and configuration"
```

4. **Create a Remote Repository:**
   Use platforms like GitHub, GitLab, or Bitbucket to host your repository and push your changes:

```bash
```

```
git remote add origin
https://github.com/yourusername/your-repo.git
git push -u origin master
```

Debugging Tools

Debugging is an inevitable part of development. Here are some tools and techniques to help you troubleshoot issues:

- **Built-in Debuggers:**
  Both VSCode and PyCharm come with integrated debuggers that allow you to set breakpoints, step through code, and inspect variables.
- **Logging:**
  As seen in our configuration setup, logging is a critical practice. Use different logging levels (DEBUG, INFO, WARNING, ERROR) to monitor the behavior of your application.
- **Python Debugger (pdb):**
  For quick debugging sessions directly from the command line, you can use Python's built-in debugger:

```python
import pdb

def example_function():
    x = 10
    pdb.set_trace()  # Execution will pause here
    y = x * 2
    return y

print(example_function())
```

Testing Frameworks

Ensuring that your code works as expected is essential. Here are a few testing frameworks that are commonly used in Python projects:

- **pytest:**
  A simple and scalable testing framework that supports fixtures,

parameterized testing, and plugins.
Installation:

```bash
pip install pytest
```

Example Test (test_graph.py):

```python
import langgraph

def test_add_node():
    graph = langgraph.Graph()
    graph.add_node("Test")
    assert "Test" in graph.nodes

def test_add_edge():
    graph = langgraph.Graph()
    graph.add_node("A")
    graph.add_node("B")
    graph.add_edge("A", "B")
    assert ("A", "B") in graph.edges

if __name__ == "__main__":
    import pytest
    pytest.main()
```

- **unittest:**
  Python's built-in testing framework, which is also a viable option for structured test cases.

Best Practices

- **Environment Isolation:**
  Always use a virtual environment to manage project dependencies. This avoids conflicts with system-wide packages.
- **Consistent Coding Standards:**
  Adopt a coding style guide such as PEP 8 for Python. Tools like `flake8` and `black` can help enforce code style and formatting.

- **Regular Commits and Branching:**
  Make small, frequent commits and use feature branches to keep your codebase organized and maintainable.
- **Automated Testing:**
  Integrate testing into your development workflow. Consider using continuous integration (CI) tools like GitHub Actions or Travis CI to automate tests on every commit.
- **Documentation:**
  Write clear and concise documentation for your code and configuration files. This not only helps others understand your work but also serves as a valuable reference for future you.

With your environment now set up, you are ready to start building autonomous AI agents using LangGraph. This chapter has covered the essential prerequisites, installation steps, and tools that will support you throughout the development process. In the next chapter, we'll dive into the core concepts and architecture of LangGraph, laying the groundwork for designing and implementing your first autonomous agent.

Chapter 3: Understanding LangGraph: Core Concepts and Architecture

In this chapter, we delve into the fundamental concepts and architecture of LangGraph. We start by exploring basic graph theory concepts that underpin LangGraph, then take an in-depth look at its internal architecture, and finally examine how LangGraph integrates with machine learning libraries and other AI frameworks. This knowledge will provide you with the foundation to build sophisticated autonomous AI agents.

3.1 Graph Fundamentals

Graph theory is the mathematical study of networks of nodes (also called vertices) connected by edges (or links). In LangGraph, these principles are harnessed to model relationships, workflows, and complex data structures in a clear and flexible way.

Key Concepts in Graph Theory

- **Nodes (Vertices):**
  The individual elements or points in a graph. In the context of autonomous agents, nodes can represent states, actions, or pieces of information.
- **Edges (Links):**
  The connections between nodes. They can represent relationships, transitions, or data flow. Edges can be:
    - **Directed:** Indicating a one-way relationship (e.g., from a "start" node to a "process" node).
    - **Undirected:** Indicating a bidirectional or symmetric relationship.
    - **Weighted:** Carrying a value (or weight) that can represent cost, probability, or importance.
- **Graph Types:**
  Depending on the use case, you may encounter different types of graphs. The following table summarizes some common types:

Graph Type	Description	Relevance in LangGraph
Undirected Graph	Connections have no inherent directionality.	Useful for modeling symmetric relationships where direction isn't critical.
Directed Graph	Edges have a defined direction (from source to target).	Ideal for representing workflows, decision trees, or process flows.
Weighted Graph	Each edge is assigned a weight.	Useful when modeling costs, distances, or probabilities in decision-making.

Simple Graph Example Using LangGraph

Let's look at a basic example to demonstrate how LangGraph leverages these concepts. The following code snippet creates a simple directed, weighted graph:

```python
import langgraph

# Create a new LangGraph instance
graph = langgraph.Graph()

# Add nodes representing different steps in a
process
graph.add_node("Start")
graph.add_node("Process Data")
graph.add_node("Make Decision")

# Connect the nodes with directed edges, optionally
adding a weight to the edge
graph.add_edge("Start", "Process Data", weight=1.0)
graph.add_edge("Process Data", "Make Decision",
weight=2.5)

# Display the graph's structure
print("Graph Nodes:", graph.nodes)
```

```
print("Graph Edges:", graph.edges)
```

Explanation:

- **Node Creation:**
  Three nodes ("Start", "Process Data", and "Make Decision") are added to the graph.
- **Edge Creation:**
  Directed edges connect the nodes in sequence, with weights that could represent processing time or priority.
- **Output:**
  The graph's nodes and edges are printed, confirming that the relationships have been set up correctly.

This example illustrates the simplicity with which you can model complex relationships using LangGraph, setting the stage for more advanced applications.

3.2 LangGraph Architecture

Understanding LangGraph's internal architecture is essential for leveraging its full capabilities. LangGraph is designed with modularity and scalability in mind, enabling developers to build complex systems without getting bogged down by implementation details.

Core Components and Modules

LangGraph is composed of several key modules, each handling specific responsibilities:

Module	Description
Graph Engine	Manages the creation, manipulation, and deletion of nodes and edges.
Node Manager	Handles node-specific operations, including data storage and metadata management.
Edge Manager	Oversees the establishment and maintenance of relationships between nodes.

Module	Description
Query Engine	Provides APIs for traversing, searching, and analyzing the graph structure.
Configuration Handler	Manages configuration settings for both the graph and integrated agents.

Internal Data Structures

At its core, LangGraph uses simple yet powerful data structures:

- **Nodes:** Typically represented as objects or dictionaries containing properties (e.g., unique ID, data payload).
- **Edges:** Stored as tuples or objects containing source and target node references, and optionally, a weight or additional metadata.

This design ensures that graph operations remain efficient and that the system can easily scale to accommodate larger datasets.

Execution Flow

1. **Initialization:**
   The graph is initialized, setting up the underlying data structures and loading any default configuration.
2. **Node and Edge Operations:**
   Developers add nodes and edges through straightforward API calls, which are managed by the Node and Edge Managers.
3. **Query Processing:**
   When a query is issued (for example, traversing the graph to find a path), the Query Engine processes the request using optimized algorithms.
4. **Integration and Extensions:**
   Custom modules or third-party integrations can be plugged into the system, thanks to LangGraph's modular architecture.

Custom Module Example

Suppose you want to extend LangGraph by adding a custom module that logs every time a new node is added. You might implement it as follows:

```python
```

```python
class NodeLogger:
    def __init__(self, graph):
        self.graph = graph
        self.log = []

    def on_node_added(self, node):
        message = f"Node added: {node}"
        self.log.append(message)
        print(message)

# Create a graph instance
graph = langgraph.Graph()

# Initialize and attach the custom NodeLogger
module
node_logger = NodeLogger(graph)
graph.register_callback("node_added",
node_logger.on_node_added)

# Add a node to see the logger in action
graph.add_node("LoggedNode")
```

Explanation:

- **NodeLogger Class:**
  A custom class that logs a message every time a node is added.
- **Callback Registration:**
  The logger is registered as a callback for the "node_added" event.
  Now, whenever `graph.add_node()` is called, the logger will
  print and store a message.
- **Demonstration:**
  Adding the node "LoggedNode" triggers the callback, demonstrating
  the extensibility of LangGraph's architecture.

3.3 Integration with AI and Machine Learning

LangGraph is not just a tool for managing graph data structures—it is also
designed to work seamlessly with AI and machine learning frameworks. This
integration allows you to incorporate graph-based representations into your

machine learning pipelines, enhancing data processing, feature extraction, and decision-making processes.

Interfacing with Machine Learning Libraries

LangGraph can be integrated with popular machine learning libraries such as TensorFlow, PyTorch, and scikit-learn. The graph structures maintained by LangGraph can serve as both data sources and organizational frameworks for model training and inference.

Example: Using LangGraph with scikit-learn

Below is a simple example that demonstrates how to extract data from a LangGraph instance and use it to train a logistic regression model with scikit-learn:

```python
python

import langgraph
import numpy as np
from sklearn.linear_model import LogisticRegression

# Create a graph instance and add nodes with
associated feature data
graph = langgraph.Graph()
graph.add_node("Node1", data={'features': [0.1,
0.2, 0.3]})
graph.add_node("Node2", data={'features': [0.4,
0.5, 0.6]})
graph.add_edge("Node1", "Node2")

# Function to retrieve node data safely
def get_node_features(graph, node_id):
    node = graph.get_node(node_id)
    return node.get('data', {}).get('features', [])

# Extract features from the nodes
features = [
    get_node_features(graph, "Node1"),
    get_node_features(graph, "Node2")
]
features = np.array(features)
```

```
# Dummy labels for training (for example purposes)
labels = [0, 1]

# Initialize and train a logistic regression model
model = LogisticRegression()
model.fit(features, labels)

# Output the model's coefficients to confirm
training
print("Model coefficients:", model.coef_)
```

Explanation:

- **Graph Data Storage:**
  Each node stores a dictionary under the key data, containing a list of feature values.
- **Feature Extraction:**
  The helper function get_node_features safely extracts the feature list from a given node.
- **Model Training:**
  The features are converted into a NumPy array and used to train a logistic regression model with scikit-learn. Dummy labels are used for simplicity.
- **Result:**
  The model's coefficients are printed, indicating that the training process has completed successfully.

Benefits of Integration

- **Data Organization:**
  Graph structures naturally organize data into interconnected nodes and edges, which can represent relationships between features or entities.
- **Feature Engineering:**
  You can derive new features based on the relationships in the graph (e.g., node degree, centrality measures) to improve model performance.
- **Dynamic Learning:**
  LangGraph's architecture allows for real-time updates to data, enabling machine learning models to be retrained or updated as new information is added.

Integration Workflow Summary

Component	Role in Integration
Data Extraction	Retrieve and preprocess data from LangGraph nodes and edges for use in ML models.
Feature Engineering	Derive new features based on graph metrics and relationships.
Model Training	Use standard machine learning libraries to train models on processed graph data.
Prediction & Feedback	Integrate predictions back into LangGraph to update agent behavior dynamically.

By integrating LangGraph with AI frameworks, developers can create adaptive systems that not only store and manage complex relationships but also learn from them, enabling sophisticated decision-making processes in autonomous AI agents.

Summary

In this chapter, we explored:

- **Graph Fundamentals:**
  The basic concepts of nodes, edges, and various graph types, along with a simple code example to illustrate these ideas.
- **LangGraph Architecture:**
  A detailed look at the modular design, core components, and internal data structures that make LangGraph both powerful and extensible. We even saw how to extend LangGraph with a custom module.
- **Integration with AI and Machine Learning:**
  How LangGraph can be seamlessly integrated with machine learning libraries, demonstrated with a scikit-learn example, and the benefits of this integration for building intelligent, autonomous agents.

With these core concepts and architectural insights, you are now better equipped to leverage LangGraph in your projects. In the next chapter, we will explore how to design autonomous AI agents, building upon the foundation established here.

Chapter 5: Implementation Details: Building Your First Autonomous Agent

In this chapter, we will bring together everything you have learned so far and build your first autonomous AI agent using LangGraph. We will walk through every step—from project setup and planning to writing code and finally debugging and testing your agent. By the end of this chapter, you will have a working prototype of an autonomous agent and a solid understanding of how to iterate on your design.

5.1 Project Setup and Planning

Before writing any code, it's crucial to carefully plan your project. A well-structured plan will help you keep your code organized, simplify debugging, and make future enhancements easier. In this section, we cover defining requirements, planning the agent's features, and setting up your project structure.

Defining Requirements

Start by outlining what your autonomous agent should do. For example, let's say we want to build an agent that:

- **Monitors Input Data:** Reads data from a source (this could be user input, sensor data, or messages).
- **Processes Data:** Analyzes the data and determines a course of action.
- **Makes Decisions:** Uses a graph-based structure to choose from a set of actions.
- **Logs Activities:** Keeps a record of decisions and data flow for further analysis.

Below is a simple table summarizing the core requirements:

Requirement	Description
Input Monitoring	The agent listens for incoming data or commands.

Requirement	Description
Data Processing	The agent processes the data using predefined logic and graph structures.
Decision Making	The agent chooses the next step based on conditions defined in the graph.
Activity Logging	The agent logs its actions for debugging and performance tracking.

Planning the Agent's Features

Based on these requirements, plan the key features and components of your agent. Here are some features we will implement:

- **Graph Initialization:** Create a graph with nodes representing different states or actions.
- **Event Handling:** Define events that trigger transitions between nodes.
- **Decision Logic:** Use simple conditions or rules that determine how the agent moves from one node to another.
- **Logging:** Implement logging to record agent activities and decisions.

Setting Up the Project Structure

Organize your project files in a clear directory structure. A recommended structure might look like this:

```bash

autonomous_agent_project/
├── env/                     # Virtual environment
directory
├── src/
│   ├── __init__.py
│   ├── agent.py             # Contains the agent
class and logic
│   ├── graph_config.yaml    # Configuration file
for the graph
│   └── utils.py             # Helper functions and
utilities
├── tests/
│   ├── __init__.py
```

```
|     └── test_agent.py          # Automated tests for
your agent
├── requirements.txt          # List of dependencies
(e.g., langgraph, pyyaml)
└── README.md                 # Project overview and
setup instructions
```

Explanation:

- **src/**: Contains your source code including the main agent logic, configuration files, and utility scripts.
- **tests/**: Holds test scripts to verify that your agent works as expected.
- **requirements.txt**: Lists all external dependencies for easy installation.
- **README.md**: Provides instructions and an overview of the project.

5.2 Step-by-Step Coding Walkthrough

Now that you have planned your project, let's build the autonomous agent step by step. In this section, we will create an agent that initializes a graph, processes input events, makes decisions, and logs activities.

Step 1: Initializing the Agent and Graph

Create a new Python file in the `src/` directory named `agent.py`. Start by importing necessary modules and initializing your LangGraph instance.

```python
# src/agent.py

import langgraph
import yaml
import logging

# Load configuration for the graph (from a YAML
file)
def load_config(file_path='src/graph_config.yaml'):
    with open(file_path, 'r') as file:
        config = yaml.safe_load(file)
```

```python
    return config

# Initialize logging based on a simple
configuration
logging.basicConfig(
    filename='agent.log',
    level=logging.INFO,
    format='%(asctime)s - %(levelname)s -
%(message)s'
)

class AutonomousAgent:
    def __init__(self, config):
        self.config = config
        self.graph =
langgraph.Graph(layout=config.get('graph',
{}).get('default_layout', 'spring'))
        self.setup_graph()

    def setup_graph(self):
        # Define nodes representing different agent
states
        self.graph.add_node("Idle")
        self.graph.add_node("Processing")
        self.graph.add_node("DecisionMaking")
        self.graph.add_node("Action")

        # Define edges to represent transitions
        self.graph.add_edge("Idle", "Processing")
        self.graph.add_edge("Processing",
"DecisionMaking")
        self.graph.add_edge("DecisionMaking",
"Action")
        self.graph.add_edge("Action", "Idle")

        logging.info("Graph setup complete with
nodes and edges: %s", self.graph.nodes)

    def process_input(self, data):
        # Simulate processing input data
        logging.info("Received data: %s", data)
```

```python
        # Here, you would add data processing
logic.
        return "Processed Data"

    def make_decision(self, processed_data):
        # Simple decision-making logic based on
processed data
        decision = "Action" if "trigger" in
processed_data else "Idle"
        logging.info("Decision made: %s", decision)
        return decision

    def execute_action(self, decision):
        # Execute an action based on the decision
        logging.info("Executing action: %s",
decision)
        # Action execution logic can be expanded
here.
        return f"Executed {decision}"

    def run(self, data):
        # Overall workflow for the agent
        logging.info("Agent run started.")
        processed = self.process_input(data)
        decision = self.make_decision(processed)
        result = self.execute_action(decision)
        logging.info("Agent run completed with
result: %s", result)
        return result

# For standalone testing of the agent
if __name__ == "__main__":
    config = load_config()
    agent = AutonomousAgent(config)
    # Simulate receiving some data that includes a
trigger keyword
    sample_data = "incoming data with trigger
event"
    outcome = agent.run(sample_data)
    print("Agent Outcome:", outcome)
```

Explanation:

- **Configuration Loading:**
  The `load_config` function reads a YAML configuration file
  (`graph_config.yaml`) to load settings for the graph. This file
  may contain settings like the default layout or other graph
  parameters.
- **Logging Setup:**
  We configure logging to write messages to `agent.log` with
  timestamps and log levels.
- **Agent Initialization:**
  The `AutonomousAgent` class initializes with the configuration and
  sets up a graph with nodes representing different states (e.g., "Idle",
  "Processing", etc.) and edges representing transitions between these
  states.
- **Processing, Decision Making, and Action Execution:**
  The agent methods `process_input`, `make_decision`, and
  `execute_action` simulate the workflow:
  - **process_input:** Processes incoming data.
  - **make_decision:** Makes a decision based on processed data.
    In this simple example, if the string "trigger" is found in the
    data, it moves to an "Action" state.
  - **execute_action:** Performs an action based on the decision and
    then loops back to the "Idle" state.
- **Running the Agent:**
  The `run` method ties all these steps together, logging each stage and
  returning the final outcome.

Step 2: Creating the Graph Configuration File

Create a file named `graph_config.yaml` inside the `src/` directory with
the following content:

yaml

```
# src/graph_config.yaml
graph:
  default_layout: "spring"
  max_nodes: 50

agent:
```

```
name: "SimpleAutonomousAgent"
behavior_mode: "reactive"
```

Explanation:

- **Graph Section:**
  Sets the default layout for the graph visualization and a maximum
  node limit.
- **Agent Section:**
  Defines the name and behavior mode of the agent, which could be
  used later to adjust processing logic.

Step 3: Running and Verifying Your Agent

Run your agent by executing the following command in your terminal
(ensure your virtual environment is activated):

```bash
python src/agent.py
```

You should see output similar to:

```yaml
Agent Outcome: Executed Action
```

Additionally, check the `agent.log` file to verify that each step of the
agent's workflow was logged correctly.

5.3 Debugging, Testing, and Iteration

After implementing your autonomous agent, it's essential to ensure that it
works correctly. This section covers strategies for debugging, testing, and
iterating on your design.

Debugging Techniques

1. **Logging:**
   As seen in our implementation, logging provides real-time feedback

on what your agent is doing. Ensure that logging levels (DEBUG, INFO, WARNING, ERROR) are appropriately set to capture necessary information.

2. **Breakpoints and Interactive Debuggers:**
Use the built-in Python debugger (pdb) or integrated debuggers in IDEs like VSCode or PyCharm to pause execution and inspect variables. For example:

```python
import pdb

def process_input(self, data):
    pdb.set_trace()  # Execution will pause here
    logging.info("Received data: %s", data)
    return "Processed Data"
```

3. **Print Statements:**
Although less sophisticated, temporary print statements can be useful during early development phases.

Testing Your Agent

Automated testing ensures that changes do not break existing functionality. Create tests in the tests/ directory. For example, create a file named test_agent.py:

```python
# tests/test_agent.py

import pytest
from src.agent import AutonomousAgent, load_config

@pytest.fixture
def agent():
    config = load_config('src/graph_config.yaml')
    return AutonomousAgent(config)

def test_process_input(agent):
    sample_input = "test input without trigger"
```

```python
    result = agent.process_input(sample_input)
    # In our simple example, the processing always
returns "Processed Data"
    assert result == "Processed Data"

def test_make_decision_idle(agent):
    # Test decision when no trigger is present in
processed data
    decision = agent.make_decision("Processed
Data")
    assert decision == "Idle"

def test_make_decision_action(agent):
    # Test decision when a trigger is present
    decision = agent.make_decision("Processed Data
with trigger")
    assert decision == "Action"

def test_run(agent):
    # Run the full agent process and verify the
outcome
    outcome = agent.run("input with trigger event")
    assert "Executed" in outcome

if __name__ == '__main__':
    pytest.main()
```

Explanation:

- **Fixtures:**
  We use a `pytest` fixture to initialize the `AutonomousAgent` instance.
- **Test Cases:**
  Separate test functions validate different methods of the agent. These tests ensure that:
  - The `process_input` method returns the expected result.
  - The `make_decision` method selects the correct state based on input.
  - The full `run` method behaves as expected.

Iteration and Continuous Improvement

Developing an autonomous agent is an iterative process. Here are some best practices to iterate on your design:

- **Collect Feedback:**
  Use logs and test results to identify areas where the agent's behavior can be improved.
- **Refactor Code:**
  Regularly review and refactor your code to improve readability, performance, and maintainability.
- **Enhance Features:**
  Once your basic agent is working, consider adding more advanced features such as:
  - Improved decision-making logic (e.g., using machine learning for predictions).
  - Additional nodes and transitions to cover more complex workflows.
  - Enhanced error handling and resilience.
- **Integrate Continuous Integration (CI):**
  Tools like GitHub Actions, Travis CI, or CircleCI can automate testing every time you make a change, ensuring your code remains stable.

Summary

In this chapter, you learned how to build your first autonomous agent using LangGraph by:

1. **Project Setup and Planning:**
   - Defining clear requirements.
   - Planning features and establishing a robust project structure.
2. **Step-by-Step Coding Walkthrough:**
   - Initializing the agent and graph.
   - Writing modular code to process input, make decisions, and execute actions.
   - Creating and using a configuration file to manage settings.
3. **Debugging, Testing, and Iteration:**
   - Employing effective debugging techniques such as logging, breakpoints, and interactive debugging.
   - Writing automated tests to verify that each component works as expected.

o   Iteratively improving the agent based on feedback and testing.

With these implementation details, you now have a complete, working example of an autonomous agent. Use this foundation as a starting point, and feel free to expand on it to build more complex and intelligent systems.

Chapter 6: Advanced Techniques and Optimization

As you become more comfortable with LangGraph and autonomous agents, you may encounter scenarios that require enhanced performance, scalability, or even custom functionality beyond the built-in capabilities. In this chapter, we explore advanced techniques for optimizing your applications, scaling your systems, and extending LangGraph to better meet your project's needs. Each section is designed to provide practical advice, clear examples, and actionable strategies to elevate your development efforts.

6.1 Performance Tuning in LangGraph

Performance is critical in systems where real-time decisions and large-scale data processing are required. In LangGraph, several techniques can be used to optimize graph queries, improve response times, and handle complex operations efficiently.

Optimizing Graph Queries

Graph queries are central to LangGraph, and optimizing these queries can significantly improve performance. Consider the following strategies:

- **Indexing:**
  Just as with traditional databases, indexing nodes or frequently queried properties can speed up search operations.
- **Query Optimization:**
  Use efficient traversal algorithms and limit the scope of searches. For example, when searching for a particular node, restrict the query to a subgraph if possible.
- **Lazy Loading:**
  Instead of loading the entire graph into memory, load only the relevant sections needed for a particular query.

Example: Optimized Graph Query

Imagine you have a large graph representing network nodes, and you want to quickly find nodes connected to a given node. Here's an example of how you might optimize this query:

python

```
# Assume langgraph supports an indexing method for
nodes
import langgraph

# Create and populate a large graph
graph = langgraph.Graph()
for i in range(1000):
    graph.add_node(f"Node{i}")

# Create edges in a structured way
for i in range(990):
    graph.add_edge(f"Node{i}", f"Node{i+1}")

# Index nodes based on a key property (if
available)
graph.create_index(property_name="id")

# Optimized query: find immediate neighbors of a
specific node
def get_neighbors(node_id):
    # Using an indexed lookup for fast retrieval
    node = graph.find_node_by_property("id",
node_id)
    return graph.get_adjacent_nodes(node)

neighbors = get_neighbors("Node500")
print("Neighbors of Node500:", neighbors)
```

Explanation:

- **Index Creation:**
  The create_index method (hypothetically provided by LangGraph) is used to index nodes by a specific property.

- **Indexed Query:**
  The `find_node_by_property` method allows for a fast lookup, and `get_adjacent_nodes` retrieves connected nodes efficiently.

Caching Strategies

Caching can drastically reduce computation time by storing results of expensive operations. In LangGraph, caching strategies might include:

- **Query Result Caching:**
  Cache the results of frequently executed queries to avoid repeated computations.
- **Edge Weight Caching:**
  If calculating edge weights is resource-intensive, cache these values to reuse them during subsequent queries.

Example: Simple Caching Implementation

Below is an example of how you might implement a simple caching mechanism for a frequently executed graph query:

```python
python

import langgraph
import functools

graph = langgraph.Graph()
# Assume nodes and edges have been added to the
graph
```

```python
# A simple cache dictionary
cache = {}

def cached_query(node_id):
    if node_id in cache:
        return cache[node_id]

    # Simulate an expensive graph query
    result =
graph.get_adjacent_nodes(graph.find_node_by_id(node
_id))
```

```
    cache[node_id] = result
    return result

# Example usage:
neighbors = cached_query("Node100")
print("Cached Neighbors of Node100:", neighbors)
```

Explanation:

- **Cache Dictionary:**
  A Python dictionary is used to store the results of queries keyed by node IDs.
- **Cache Check:**
  Before executing the query, the function checks if the result is already available in the cache.
- **Result Storage:**
  If the result is not cached, the query is executed, and the result is stored for future use.

Parallel Processing for Real-Time Performance

When dealing with large datasets or computationally heavy tasks, parallel processing can significantly enhance performance. Python's built-in modules such as `multiprocessing` or third-party libraries like `joblib` can help distribute the workload.

Example: Using Multiprocessing

Below is an example demonstrating how to perform parallel processing on graph queries using the `multiprocessing` module:

python

```
import langgraph
from multiprocessing import Pool

# Function to perform a graph operation
def process_node(node_id):
    node = graph.find_node_by_id(node_id)
    # Simulate a complex operation (e.g., computing
centrality)
```

```
    return (node_id,
len(graph.get_adjacent_nodes(node)))

# Create a graph and add nodes
graph = langgraph.Graph()
for i in range(1000):
    graph.add_node(f"Node{i}")
    if i > 0:
        graph.add_edge(f"Node{i-1}", f"Node{i}")

# Create a pool of worker processes
with Pool(processes=4) as pool:
    node_ids = [f"Node{i}" for i in range(1000)]
    results = pool.map(process_node, node_ids)

# Display a sample of the results
print("Sample parallel processing results:",
results[:10])
```

Explanation:

- **Process Pool:**
  A pool of worker processes is created to handle tasks concurrently.
- **Mapping Function:**
  The `process_node` function is applied to each node ID in parallel using `pool.map`, which distributes the workload.
- **Result Collection:**
  Results are gathered and can be used to further analyze the performance of graph operations.

6.2 Scalability

Scaling autonomous agents to handle larger datasets and more complex interactions is a common challenge. Here, we discuss strategies to ensure that your LangGraph-based applications can grow as needed.

Vertical and Horizontal Scaling

- **Vertical Scaling:**
  Involves upgrading the hardware (e.g., more powerful CPU, additional memory) on which your agent runs.
- **Horizontal Scaling:**
  Involves distributing the workload across multiple machines or processes. This is particularly useful when dealing with large graphs that cannot be efficiently processed on a single machine.

Strategies for Scaling Autonomous Agents

Strategy	Description	Example/Application
Sharding:	Partitioning the graph into smaller, more manageable pieces.	Divide a social network graph by region or user group.
Distributed Processing:	Using multiple machines or nodes to process different parts of the graph concurrently.	Utilizing clusters or cloud services like AWS or Google Cloud.
Load Balancing:	Distributing incoming requests evenly across multiple agents or servers.	Implementing a load balancer to manage web requests.
Caching and Preprocessing:	Precompute common queries and store results for fast access.	Cache results of frequent computations in a distributed cache (e.g., Redis).

Example: Sharding a Graph

Suppose you need to partition a large graph into smaller subgraphs for distributed processing. Here's a simple conceptual example:

```python
import langgraph

def shard_graph(graph, shard_size):
    nodes = list(graph.nodes)
    shards = []
```

```
    for i in range(0, len(nodes), shard_size):
        shard = langgraph.Graph()
        for node in nodes[i:i + shard_size]:
            shard.add_node(node)
            # Copy edges if both nodes are in the
current shard
            for adjacent in
graph.get_adjacent_nodes(node):
                if adjacent in shard.nodes:
                    shard.add_edge(node, adjacent)
        shards.append(shard)
    return shards

# Create a large graph
graph = langgraph.Graph()
for i in range(1000):
    graph.add_node(f"Node{i}")
    if i > 0:
        graph.add_edge(f"Node{i-1}", f"Node{i}")

# Partition the graph into shards of 100 nodes each
shards = shard_graph(graph, 100)
print("Number of shards created:", len(shards))
```

Explanation:

- **Graph Sharding:**
  The `shard_graph` function divides the graph's nodes into smaller groups (shards) based on the specified shard size.
- **Edge Management:**
  When copying edges, the function checks if both nodes of an edge belong to the same shard before adding the edge.

Distributed Processing Considerations

For large-scale applications, consider using cloud-based solutions or distributed computing frameworks such as Apache Spark or Dask. These platforms can process large graphs in parallel across many machines.

6.3 Extending LangGraph

One of the strengths of LangGraph is its extensibility. In this section, we discuss how to create custom modules, integrate third-party APIs, and contribute to the LangGraph ecosystem.

Creating Custom Modules

Custom modules allow you to add new functionality tailored to your application's needs. For example, you might want to create a module that analyzes graph centrality or integrates specialized logging.

Example: Custom Centrality Calculator Module

```python
class CentralityCalculator:
    def __init__(self, graph):
        self.graph = graph

    def calculate_degree_centrality(self):
        centrality = {}
        for node in self.graph.nodes:
            # Degree centrality: number of adjacent
nodes
            centrality[node] =
len(self.graph.get_adjacent_nodes(node))
        return centrality

# Usage example:
graph = langgraph.Graph()
graph.add_node("A")
graph.add_node("B")
graph.add_node("C")
graph.add_edge("A", "B")
graph.add_edge("B", "C")
graph.add_edge("C", "A")

centrality_calculator = CentralityCalculator(graph)
centrality =
centrality_calculator.calculate_degree_centrality()
print("Degree Centrality:", centrality)
```

Explanation:

- **Custom Class:**
  The `CentralityCalculator` class is defined to compute the degree centrality of nodes.
- **Method:**
  The `calculate_degree_centrality` method iterates through all nodes, counts the adjacent nodes, and stores the result.
- **Usage:**
  After setting up a simple graph, the custom module is used to calculate and print the degree centrality for each node.

Integrating Third-Party APIs

LangGraph can be integrated with third-party APIs to extend functionality. For example, you might integrate a weather API into an agent that makes decisions based on weather data.

Example: Integrating a Weather API

Below is a simplified example that shows how you might incorporate data from a weather API into your agent workflow:

```python
import requests

def get_weather_data(location):
    api_key = "YOUR_API_KEY"
    url = f"https://api.weatherapi.com/v1/current.json?key={api_key}&q={location}"
    response = requests.get(url)
    if response.status_code == 200:
        return response.json()  # Returns a dictionary with weather information
    else:
        return None

# Example usage:
weather_info = get_weather_data("New York")
if weather_info:
```

```
    current_temp =
weather_info['current']['temp_c']
    print(f"Current temperature in New York:
{current_temp}°C")
else:
    print("Failed to retrieve weather data.")
```

Explanation:

- **API Request:**
  The get_weather_data function makes an HTTP GET request to a weather API using the requests library.
- **Data Handling:**
  The function checks the response status, parses the JSON response if successful, and returns weather information.
- **Usage:**
  The example demonstrates retrieving and printing the current temperature for a specified location.

Contributing to the LangGraph Ecosystem

LangGraph's open architecture encourages contributions from the community. Here are some ways to get involved:

- **Custom Module Libraries:**
  Share your custom modules with the community by contributing to open-source repositories or LangGraph-related projects.
- **API Integrations:**
  Develop and document integrations with popular third-party APIs.
- **Bug Fixes and Enhancements:**
  Contribute to the LangGraph codebase by fixing bugs, adding features, or improving documentation. Follow the project's contribution guidelines on its repository.
- **Community Forums and Tutorials:**
  Engage with other developers in forums, write tutorials, or create demo projects to showcase innovative uses of LangGraph.

Summary

In this chapter, we explored advanced techniques and optimization strategies for building high-performance, scalable autonomous agents with LangGraph:

- **Performance Tuning:**
  - Optimized graph queries through indexing, lazy loading, and efficient traversal.
  - Implemented caching strategies to store expensive query results.
  - Leveraged parallel processing using Python's `multiprocessing` module to handle large datasets in real time.
- **Scalability:**
  - Discussed vertical and horizontal scaling strategies.
  - Demonstrated sharding techniques and provided a table summarizing key scaling strategies.
  - Introduced considerations for distributed processing using cloud or cluster-based solutions.
- **Extending LangGraph:**
  - Showed how to create custom modules, such as a centrality calculator.
  - Explained the integration of third-party APIs with a practical weather API example.
  - Provided guidance on contributing to the LangGraph ecosystem through community engagement and code contributions.

By applying these advanced techniques, you can enhance the performance, scalability, and functionality of your autonomous agents, ensuring they can meet the demands of increasingly complex real-world applications. Happy coding, and keep pushing the boundaries of what you can build with LangGraph!

Chapter 7: Case Studies and Real-World Applications

In this chapter, we explore two comprehensive case studies that demonstrate how LangGraph can be used to build autonomous AI agents in real-world scenarios. We'll walk through the development of an **Autonomous Customer Support Agent** and an **Intelligent Data Analysis Agent**. Finally, we summarize the lessons learned and best practices from these implementations to help guide you in your own projects.

7.1 Case Study 1: Autonomous Customer Support Agent

Customer support is a prime application for autonomous AI agents. In this case study, we examine an agent designed to handle customer inquiries, provide immediate solutions, or escalate issues when necessary. By leveraging LangGraph, the agent is structured as a state machine with nodes representing various stages of a customer interaction.

Design Overview

The support agent's workflow is mapped out as a graph with the following key nodes:

Node	Description
Greeting	Welcomes the customer and initiates the conversation.
IssueIdentification	Collects information about the customer's problem.
Solution	Provides a solution based on the information gathered.
Escalation	Escalates the issue to a human agent if the problem is urgent.
Farewell	Concludes the conversation courteously.

Implementation Details

Below is a complete Python example demonstrating how to implement the Autonomous Customer Support Agent using LangGraph:

```python
python

# src/customer_support_agent.py

import langgraph
import logging

# Set up logging for the agent
logging.basicConfig(
    filename='customer_support_agent.log',
    level=logging.INFO,
    format='%(asctime)s - %(levelname)s -
%(message)s'
)

class CustomerSupportAgent:
    def __init__(self):
        self.graph = langgraph.Graph()
        self.setup_graph()

    def setup_graph(self):
        """
        Define the conversation flow by adding
nodes and edges.
        """
        # Add nodes representing different states
        self.graph.add_node("Greeting")
        self.graph.add_node("IssueIdentification")
        self.graph.add_node("Solution")
        self.graph.add_node("Escalation")
        self.graph.add_node("Farewell")

        # Define transitions between the states
        self.graph.add_edge("Greeting",
"IssueIdentification")
        self.graph.add_edge("IssueIdentification",
"Solution")
        self.graph.add_edge("IssueIdentification",
"Escalation")
        self.graph.add_edge("Solution", "Farewell")
        self.graph.add_edge("Escalation",
"Farewell")
```

```python
        logging.info("Customer Support Agent graph
initialized with nodes: %s", self.graph.nodes)

    def handle_query(self, query):
        """
        Process the customer query and decide
whether to provide a solution or escalate.
        """
        logging.info("Received query: %s", query)
        # Simple decision logic: if the query
contains "urgent", escalate; otherwise, provide a
solution.
        if "urgent" in query.lower():
            decision = "Escalation"
        else:
            decision = "Solution"
        logging.info("Decision made: %s", decision)
        return decision

    def run(self, query):
        """
        Simulate a conversation with the customer.
        """
        print("Agent: Hello! How can I help you
today?")
        # Transition from Greeting to
IssueIdentification
        logging.info("Transition: Greeting ->
IssueIdentification")
        decision = self.handle_query(query)
        # Follow the decision branch
        if decision == "Solution":
            print("Agent: I suggest restarting your
device. Has that resolved your issue?")
        elif decision == "Escalation":
            print("Agent: I will escalate this
issue to our technical team immediately.")
        # Transition to Farewell
        logging.info("Transition: %s -> Farewell",
decision)
```

```
        print("Agent: Thank you for contacting
support. Have a great day!")

# For standalone testing
if __name__ == "__main__":
    agent = CustomerSupportAgent()
    # Simulate a query from a customer
    sample_query = "I'm having an urgent problem
with my internet connection."
    agent.run(sample_query)
```

Explanation

1. **Graph Initialization:**
   The agent initializes a LangGraph instance and defines a
   conversation flow by adding nodes for "Greeting",
   "IssueIdentification", "Solution", "Escalation", and "Farewell".
   Transitions (edges) connect these nodes to form a state machine.
2. **Handling Queries:**
   The `handle_query` method processes incoming customer queries.
   It uses simple keyword matching (e.g., checking for the word
   "urgent") to decide whether to escalate the issue or provide a
   solution.
3. **Running the Agent:**
   The `run` method simulates the conversation by printing messages to
   the console and logging each transition. This method ties together the
   entire process, from greeting to farewell.

This case study demonstrates how you can use LangGraph to create an
interactive, state-driven customer support agent that handles inquiries
autonomously while logging all actions for further analysis.

7.2 Case Study 2: Intelligent Data Analysis Agent

The second case study focuses on building an agent that processes and
analyzes large datasets autonomously. This agent leverages LangGraph to
manage different stages of a data analysis pipeline, from data ingestion to
reporting.

Design Overview

The data analysis pipeline is organized as a series of graph nodes, each representing a step in the process:

Node	Description
DataIngestion	Loads data from a specified source (e.g., a CSV file).
DataCleaning	Processes and cleans the data, such as handling missing values.
FeatureExtraction	Extracts relevant features from the cleaned data for model training.
ModelTraining	Trains a machine learning model on the extracted features.
Reporting	Generates a summary report based on the model's performance and data analysis.

Implementation Details

Below is a complete Python example that implements the Intelligent Data Analysis Agent using LangGraph and integrates with common data analysis libraries:

python

```python
# src/data_analysis_agent.py

import langgraph
import pandas as pd
from sklearn.linear_model import LinearRegression
import logging

# Configure logging
logging.basicConfig(
    filename='data_analysis_agent.log',
    level=logging.INFO,
    format='%(asctime)s - %(levelname)s - %(message)s'
)

class DataAnalysisAgent:
```

```python
    def __init__(self):
        self.graph = langgraph.Graph()
        self.setup_graph()

    def setup_graph(self):
        """
        Define the data analysis pipeline as a
graph.
        """
        # Add nodes for each step in the pipeline
        self.graph.add_node("DataIngestion")
        self.graph.add_node("DataCleaning")
        self.graph.add_node("FeatureExtraction")
        self.graph.add_node("ModelTraining")
        self.graph.add_node("Reporting")

        # Define the workflow transitions
        self.graph.add_edge("DataIngestion",
"DataCleaning")
        self.graph.add_edge("DataCleaning",
"FeatureExtraction")
        self.graph.add_edge("FeatureExtraction",
"ModelTraining")
        self.graph.add_edge("ModelTraining",
"Reporting")

        logging.info("Data Analysis Agent graph
initialized with nodes: %s", self.graph.nodes)

    def run(self, data_path):
        """
        Execute the data analysis pipeline.
        """
        # Step 1: Data Ingestion
        logging.info("Starting Data Ingestion.")
        data = pd.read_csv(data_path)
        print("Data Ingestion complete. Data
shape:", data.shape)

        # Step 2: Data Cleaning
        logging.info("Starting Data Cleaning.")
        data_clean = data.dropna()
```

```python
        print("Data Cleaning complete. Data
shape:", data_clean.shape)

        # Step 3: Feature Extraction
        logging.info("Starting Feature
Extraction.")
        # For simplicity, assume all numeric
columns (except 'target') are features
        features =
data_clean.select_dtypes(include=['number'])
        X = features.drop(columns=['target'],
errors='ignore')
        # If 'target' is not present, create a
dummy target variable
        y = features['target'] if 'target' in
features else pd.Series([0] * len(features))
        print("Feature Extraction complete. Number
of features:", X.shape[1])

        # Step 4: Model Training
        logging.info("Starting Model Training.")
        model = LinearRegression()
        model.fit(X, y)
        print("Model Training complete.
Coefficients:", model.coef_)

        # Step 5: Reporting
        logging.info("Starting Reporting.")
        print("Reporting complete. Data analysis
successful.")

        return model

# For standalone testing
if __name__ == "__main__":
    agent = DataAnalysisAgent()
    # Replace 'data.csv' with the path to your
dataset file
    model = agent.run('data.csv')
```

Explanation

1. **Graph Initialization:**
   The agent initializes a LangGraph instance and defines nodes for each stage of the data analysis pipeline: Data Ingestion, Data Cleaning, Feature Extraction, Model Training, and Reporting. Edges are set up to establish the order of execution.
2. **Data Pipeline Execution:**
   o **Data Ingestion:** Reads data from a CSV file using Pandas.
   o **Data Cleaning:** Removes missing values from the dataset.
   o **Feature Extraction:** Selects numeric columns (excluding the target, if present) as features for model training.
   o **Model Training:** Trains a Linear Regression model using scikit-learn.
   o **Reporting:** Outputs the results and logs each step of the process.
3. **Logging and Output:**
   The agent logs the progress of each pipeline stage and prints relevant details, ensuring transparency and ease of debugging.

This case study illustrates how LangGraph can structure and manage a complex data analysis workflow, making it easier to build scalable and maintainable data processing pipelines.

7.3 Lessons Learned and Best Practices

Drawing from these case studies, here are some key takeaways and best practices for building autonomous agents with LangGraph:

Key Lessons

- **Modular Design:**
  Breaking down the application into distinct modules (e.g., conversation states or data processing steps) simplifies both development and maintenance.
- **Clear Workflow Definition:**
  Using a graph to define workflows helps visualize transitions and dependencies between different states or processing steps.
- **Effective Logging:**
  Logging every significant step enables easy debugging and

performance monitoring. Be sure to adjust log levels appropriately for production versus development environments.

- **Simple Decision Logic:**
  Start with straightforward logic (like keyword matching) and iteratively enhance the decision-making process as you gather user feedback and operational data.
- **Robust Testing:**
  Automate tests for each module to catch errors early and ensure that changes do not disrupt existing functionalities.

Best Practices

Best Practice	Description
Plan Before Coding	Define requirements, design the workflow, and sketch out the graph structure.
Keep It Modular	Develop independent modules for each task to simplify debugging and future enhancements.
Implement Robust Logging	Log key events and transitions to diagnose issues quickly.
Automate Testing	Use unit and integration tests to verify each component of your agent.
Optimize Gradually	Start with simple implementations and iterate to improve performance and scalability.
Document Extensively	Document the code, workflows, and decisions to ensure maintainability.

Common Pitfalls

- **Overcomplicating the Workflow:**
  Avoid designing overly complex graph structures early in development. Start simple and expand as necessary.
- **Neglecting Performance Optimization:**
  As datasets or conversation logs grow, failing to implement caching or indexing can lead to performance bottlenecks.
- **Insufficient Testing:**
  Without automated tests, minor changes can introduce unexpected bugs in critical paths of the workflow.

Summary

In this chapter, we reviewed two real-world case studies demonstrating the versatility of LangGraph:

1. **Autonomous Customer Support Agent:**
   - Mapped a conversation flow with nodes representing different states.
   - Implemented decision-making logic based on customer input.
   - Emphasized the importance of logging and state transitions in a customer service context.
2. **Intelligent Data Analysis Agent:**
   - Defined a data processing pipeline with distinct stages for ingestion, cleaning, feature extraction, model training, and reporting.
   - Integrated popular libraries (Pandas, scikit-learn) to perform data analysis.
   - Highlighted how LangGraph structures complex workflows, making the process more manageable.

Finally, we summarized the lessons learned and best practices, emphasizing modular design, clear workflow definition, robust logging, automated testing, and gradual optimization. These insights can help you avoid common pitfalls and build more reliable, scalable, and efficient autonomous agents.

By applying these real-world lessons, you are better equipped to develop your own advanced autonomous systems with LangGraph.

Chapter 8: The Future of Autonomous AI Agents and LangGraph

As the field of artificial intelligence continues to evolve, so do the technologies that power autonomous agents. In this final chapter, we explore emerging trends in autonomous systems and graph-based AI, discuss how you can contribute to and engage with the LangGraph community, and offer guidance on next steps along with additional resources for continued learning.

8.1 Emerging Trends

The landscape of autonomous AI agents is rapidly evolving, driven by advancements in technology and the increasing complexity of real-world applications. Here are some key emerging trends to watch:

Graph-Based AI and Graph Neural Networks (GNNs)

- **Increased Adoption of GNNs:**
  Graph Neural Networks are gaining traction as a powerful tool for processing graph-structured data. They are being used in areas such as social network analysis, recommendation systems, fraud detection, and biological network modeling.
- **Integration with Traditional Machine Learning:**
  There is a growing trend towards hybrid models that combine graph-based representations with traditional machine learning algorithms. This fusion enhances feature extraction, improves decision-making processes, and provides deeper insights into complex data relationships.

Enhanced Autonomy in Decision-Making

- **Real-Time Adaptive Systems:**
  Future autonomous agents will increasingly incorporate real-time data feeds and adaptive algorithms that allow them to modify behavior on the fly. This includes integration with IoT devices and sensor networks for applications in smart cities, industrial automation, and autonomous vehicles.

- **Reinforcement Learning Integration:**
  Reinforcement learning (RL) techniques are being combined with graph-based approaches to enable agents to learn optimal behaviors from interactions with their environment. This synergy is particularly promising for applications that require dynamic decision-making in uncertain environments.

Scalability and Distributed Processing

- **Big Data and Distributed Computing:**
  As datasets continue to grow, scaling graph-based AI systems becomes imperative. Emerging technologies in distributed processing, such as cloud-based solutions and cluster computing frameworks (e.g., Apache Spark, Dask), are enabling real-time analytics on massive graphs.
- **Edge Computing:**
  To reduce latency and enhance performance, there is a trend toward deploying autonomous agents on edge devices. This involves optimizing models to run efficiently on hardware with limited computational resources while maintaining robust performance.

Ethics and Responsible AI

- **Transparency and Explainability:**
  With increasing reliance on autonomous systems, the demand for transparency and interpretability in AI models is on the rise. Researchers and developers are working on methods to make graph-based AI and autonomous decision-making processes more understandable to humans.
- **Ethical Considerations:**
  The deployment of autonomous agents raises important ethical questions regarding data privacy, bias, and accountability. Future developments will likely include frameworks and guidelines that ensure responsible and ethical use of AI technologies.

Below is a summary table of these emerging trends:

Trend	Description	Implications
Graph Neural Networks (GNNs)	Advanced models for processing graph-structured data.	Improved accuracy in tasks like recommendations and anomaly detection.

Trend	Description	Implications
Real-Time Adaptive Systems	Systems that adapt to changing data and conditions in real time.	Enhanced performance in dynamic environments such as IoT and robotics.
Reinforcement Learning with Graphs	Combining RL techniques with graph-based representations.	Better decision-making in uncertain and complex scenarios.
Distributed and Edge Computing	Leveraging cloud and edge devices to process large-scale data.	Scalability and reduced latency in processing autonomous tasks.
Transparency and Ethics	Increased focus on explainability, fairness, and ethical AI use.	More trust and accountability in autonomous systems.

8.2 Community and Contribution

LangGraph's success is powered not only by its innovative features but also by the vibrant and collaborative community that surrounds it. Here are some ways you can get involved:

How to Contribute

- **Open Source Contributions:**
  LangGraph is an open-source project that welcomes contributions. Whether you're fixing bugs, developing new features, or improving documentation, your efforts can help shape the future of the platform. Visit the project's GitHub repository to get started, review contribution guidelines, and submit pull requests.
- **Custom Modules and Extensions:**
  If you have developed custom modules or extensions that enhance LangGraph's capabilities (e.g., new graph algorithms, specialized data processors, or API integrations), consider sharing them with the community. Contributing your code as a separate module or a forked project can accelerate innovation.
- **Bug Reporting and Feature Requests:**
  Engage with the community by reporting bugs, suggesting enhancements, and participating in discussions. This feedback loop is essential for continuous improvement.

- **Documentation and Tutorials:**
  Comprehensive documentation is key to adoption. You can contribute by writing tutorials, creating examples, or translating documentation into other languages to help a broader audience.

Engaging with the Community

- **Forums and Mailing Lists:**
  Join LangGraph-related forums and mailing lists to discuss challenges, share ideas, and seek advice from fellow developers.
- **Online Platforms:**
  Platforms such as GitHub Discussions, Stack Overflow, and dedicated Slack or Discord channels are excellent venues for collaboration and support.
- **Meetups and Conferences:**
  Participate in or organize meetups, webinars, and conferences that focus on graph-based AI and autonomous systems. These events provide opportunities to network with experts and share your experiences.

Below is a table summarizing some of the key community engagement platforms:

Platform	Description	How to Engage
GitHub Repository	Central hub for LangGraph code, issues, and pull requests.	Contribute code, report bugs, and discuss features.
Slack/Discord Channels	Real-time communication platforms for developers.	Join channels to ask questions, share insights, and collaborate.
Stack Overflow	Q&A platform for technical questions.	Ask and answer questions related to LangGraph and graph-based AI.
Mailing Lists/Forums	Platforms for longer discussions and community announcements.	Subscribe to mailing lists and participate in forum discussions.

Platform	Description	How to Engage
Meetups/Conferences	In-person and virtual events focused on AI and technology.	Attend or organize events to network and learn from peers.

8.3 Next Steps and Additional Resources

To continue your journey in building autonomous AI agents and working with LangGraph, here are some next steps and resources that can help you expand your knowledge and skills.

Further Reading and Online Courses

Invest time in learning more about graph theory, AI, and autonomous systems. Here are some recommended resources:

Resource	Type	Description
Graph Theory and Complex Networks by Maarten van Steen	Book	A comprehensive to graph theory and its applications.
Deep Learning on Graphs by Yao Ma, et al.	Research Paper	Explores the use of deep learning techniques on graph-structured data.
Coursera – *Machine Learning* by Andrew Ng	Online Course	A foundational course that covers machine learning principles and applications.
edX – *Data Science Essentials*	Online Course	Focuses on data analysis, machine learning, and the use of Python for data science.
Udacity – *Intro to Artificial Intelligence*	Online Course	An to AI concepts, including autonomous systems and robotics.

Communities for Continued Learning

Engaging with communities can provide ongoing support, collaboration, and inspiration:

- **GitHub:** Explore repositories related to graph-based AI, contribute to projects, and follow trending topics.
- **LinkedIn Groups:** Join professional groups dedicated to AI and data science to network and exchange ideas.
- **Meetup:** Look for local or virtual meetups focused on AI, machine learning, and autonomous systems.
- **Research Conferences:** Attend conferences like NeurIPS, ICML, or KDD to stay updated on the latest research and developments.

Practical Next Steps

- **Experiment and Prototype:**
  Continue experimenting with LangGraph by building small prototypes. Tackle new challenges by extending the examples provided in this book.
- **Contribute to Open Source:**
  If you haven't already, consider contributing to the LangGraph project. Even small contributions like improving documentation or reporting bugs can have a significant impact.
- **Share Your Work:**
  Publish your projects, write blog posts, or create video tutorials to share your experiences and solutions with the broader community.

Summary

In this chapter, we looked ahead at the future of autonomous AI agents and LangGraph by discussing:

- **Emerging Trends:**
  Innovations in graph neural networks, adaptive systems, distributed processing, and ethical AI.
- **Community and Contribution:**
  Ways to engage with the LangGraph community through open source contributions, forums, and events, thereby helping shape the future of the technology.

- **Next Steps and Additional Resources:**
  Recommended readings, online courses, and community platforms to support your continuous learning and development journey.

By staying informed about emerging trends and actively participating in the community, you can play a pivotal role in advancing the field of autonomous AI agents. Continue exploring, learning, and contributing to create robust, innovative solutions that push the boundaries of what is possible with LangGraph and beyond.

Conclusion

As you reach the end of ***Building Autonomous AI Agents with LangGraph: A Developer's Guide***, I hope you feel inspired and empowered to dive deeper into the world of autonomous systems and graph-based AI. This book was designed not only to provide you with the technical know-how and practical examples needed to build robust AI agents but also to ignite your passion for innovation in a rapidly evolving field.

Throughout these chapters, we explored the fundamentals of graph theory and the internal workings of LangGraph, guiding you step by step from setting up your development environment to building, optimizing, and scaling your very own autonomous agent. We delved into real-world case studies—from a customer support agent that transforms user interactions into seamless conversations, to a data analysis agent that turns complex datasets into actionable insights—demonstrating how these concepts can be applied in diverse and impactful ways.

What makes this journey even more exciting is that it's just the beginning. The landscape of autonomous AI is continuously evolving with emerging trends such as graph neural networks, real-time adaptive systems, and ethically-driven AI practices shaping the future. Your newfound skills and insights will not only serve as a solid foundation for your own projects but also position you as a contributor to a vibrant and growing community of innovators.

I encourage you to revisit this book regularly as a source of inspiration and a technical reference. Each re-read can unveil new insights or spark fresh ideas for enhancing your projects. Your experience and feedback are vital—please share your thoughts by leaving a review, discussing your successes and challenges with peers, and contributing to community forums. Your engagement helps us all grow, innovate, and push the boundaries of what autonomous AI agents can achieve.

Thank you for embarking on this journey with me. May your projects be innovative, your code be robust, and your passion for AI continue to drive you forward. Happy coding, and we look forward to hearing how you transform these ideas into reality!

www.ingramcontent.com/pod-product-compliance
Lightning Source LLC
LaVergne TN
LVHW080119070326
832902LV00015B/2665